the very

SATISFYING

Activity Book

The Very Satisfying Activity Book. Copyright © 2020 by
St. Martin's Press. All rights reserved. Printed in China.
For information, address St. Martin's Press, 120 Broadway,
New York, NY 10271.

www.castlepointbooks.com

The Castle Point Books trademark is owned by Castle
Point Publishing, LLC. Castle Point books are published
and distributed by St. Martin's Press.

ISBN 978-1-250-27223-2 (trade paperback)

Our books may be purchased in bulk for promotional,
educational, or business use. Please contact your local
bookseller or the Macmillan Corporate and Premium Sales
Department at 1-800-221-7945, extension 5442, or
by email at MacmillanSpecialMarkets@macmillan.com.

First Edition: 2020

10 9 8 7 6 5 4 3 2 1

SATISFYING

Activity Book

Exceedingly Tidy Games and Puzzles for Perfectionists, Control Freaks, Type As, and Others Obsessed with Order

GARETH MOORE

CASTLE POINT BOOKS

NEW YORK

DOT YOUR I'S AND CROSS YOUR T'S

Satisfy your urge for order with this therapeutic seek-and-find activity. Dot any undotted i's and cross any uncrossed t's until the world makes sense again. Raise the standard by using colored pencils in just the right shades of pink and green, then bask in the glory of pure perfection.

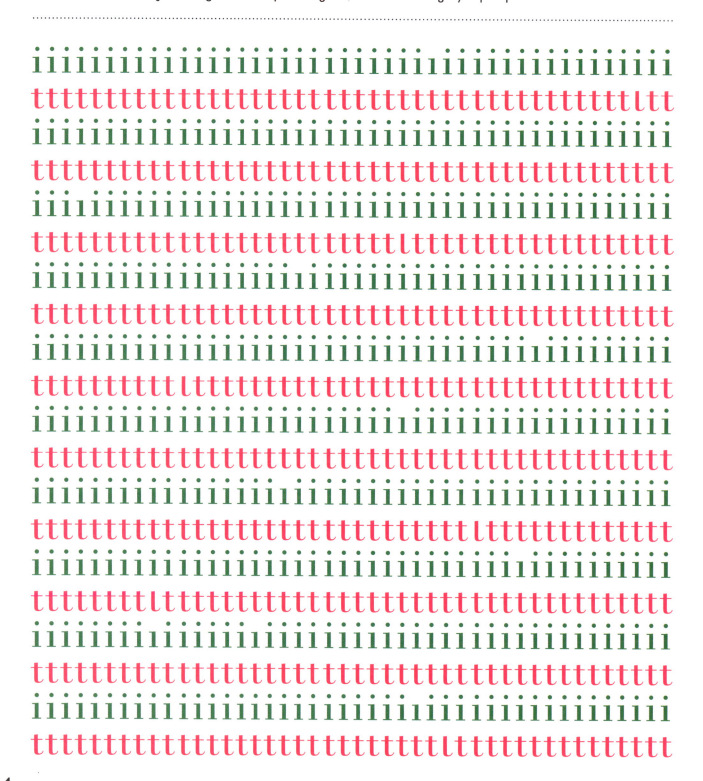

GO GREEN

You know how good it feels when you hit green lights all the way to work? Like the world is finally on your side. Simulate that incredible feeling with this happy little puzzle. There are only a few stoplights that haven't bowed to your command. Color them green and let them know who's boss of everything.

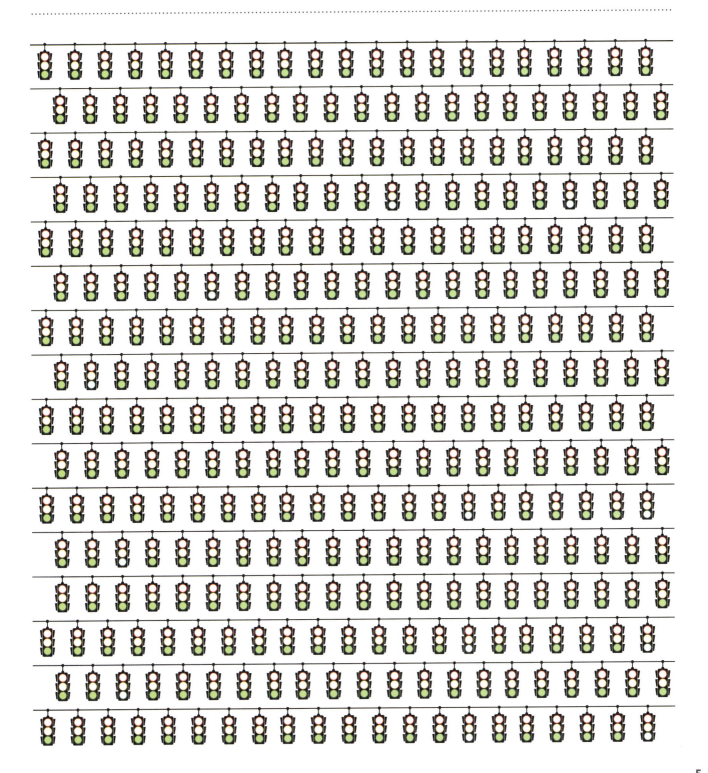

I SPY DISORDER

Imagine if your living room could always be as clean and organized as the image at left. Now compare it to the living room at right. If you're truly a type A, you'll be able to spot and circle the five blemishes that make it look a little too lived in.

FIND YOUR PIECE

Find inner peace and comfort when you locate the one shape below that (without being flipped over) can complete this image. Circle it and proceed to feel whole again.

HOSTESS WITH THE MOST-EST

Repeating patterns are the antidote to chaos. Unless, of course, they are broken by carelessness. Attend to detail and find the six place settings that threaten the integrity of this otherwise perfectly executed dinner party.

CATCH THE RAINBOWS

Most of the rainbows in this puzzle are the kind that inspire dreamers the world over. But five of them are far from perfect and must be identified and circled before they corrupt the rest.

POUR FAVOR

Whether you go through life thinking the glass is half-empty or half-full, the important thing is that it's as full as the ones next to it. Take a look at the image below and see if you can circle the five glasses that are irritatingly less full than the others.

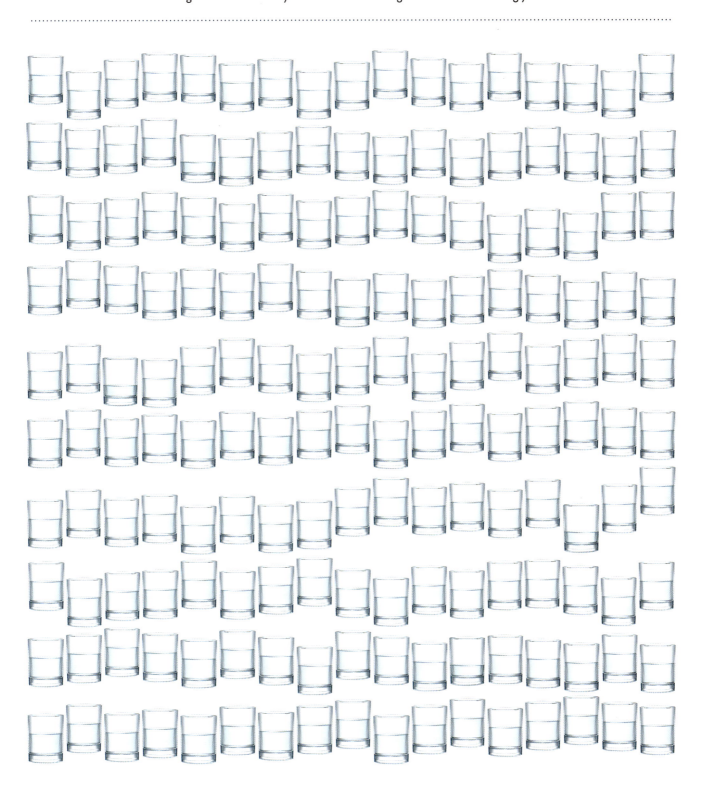

TAKE CHARGE

There are few sounds as satisfying as the chirp of a phone beginning to charge to a reassuring 100 percent. Search this page to find the five phones still losing their power. Circle each one and, as you do, imagine that you hear that satisfying chirp.

A PLACE FOR EVERYONE

Alphabetizing brings order, and order is key to any successful event. Write the names listed on the empty place cards in alphabetical order by last name. Show off that perfect handwriting!

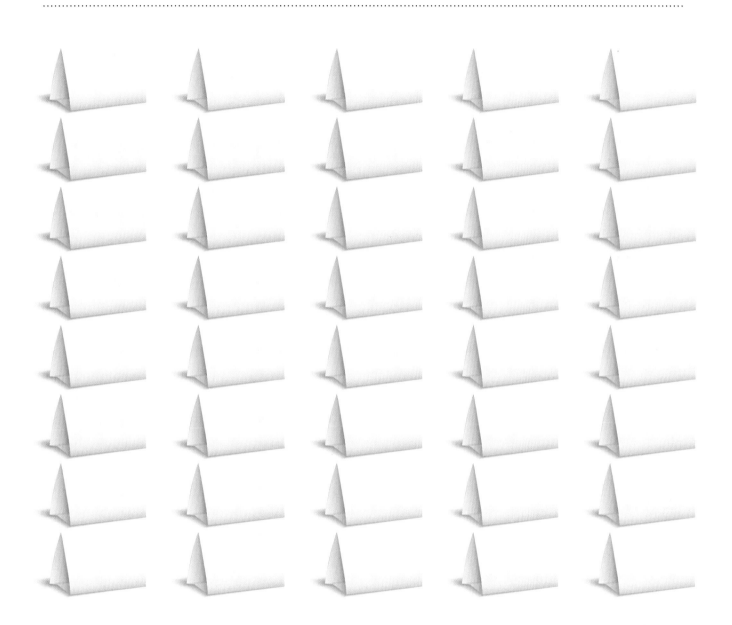

Today's guestlist is as follows:

Rees Bosley, Emmanuel Hill, Claud Gilbert, Roy Linington, Stewart Fossey, Wilfrid Course, Hugh Pare, Ivor Hancock, Peter Temby, Winnie Thompson, Harriett Fugler, Martha Kirk, Charlotte Tamblyn, Monica Treadway, Christian Lawry, Bertha Sellen, Lily Leal, Cordelia Camburn, Edith Weil, Matthew Evans, Lawrence Green, Louis Everett, Wilbur Owens, Ernest Petersen, Gerard Hooper, James Hunt, Martin Holder, Mark Ross, John Murray, Isabelle Perry, Fern Kidd, Kay Levine, Hazel Sheppard, Shari Callahan, Anne Quinn, Alisha Robles, Casey Woodard, Isabelle Navarro, Edmund Sulley, Riley Duncan

CONFECTION PERFECTION

Good caterers are difficult, but not impossible, to find—just like the five flaws in the confections at right. Satisfy your craving for perfection and use your discriminating taste to circle the five bakery fails.

COLOR CURE: LEAVES

Without color, this art feels incomplete. Use your impeccable sense of style to take this nature-inspired wallpaper from striking to breathtaking.

MAKING ARRANGEMENTS

If you've got an eye for design and symmetry, you'll appreciate this challenging drawing activity. Complete the other half of the image and imagine finding just the right spot in your home for this cheery arrangement.

DRAWN TO PERFECTION

Snowflakes remind us that perfection is possible! Recreate the missing half of these elegant
crystalline structures and applaud nature's incredibly high standards as you do so.

COOL BEANS

Numbers are neat and precise, the way life should be.
Count your way to winning a jarful of jelly beans with this delicious little puzzle.

NAILED IT

Take the perfect manicure into your own hands with this artfully satisfying activity to express your inner nail technician. Add color and style to the nails below.

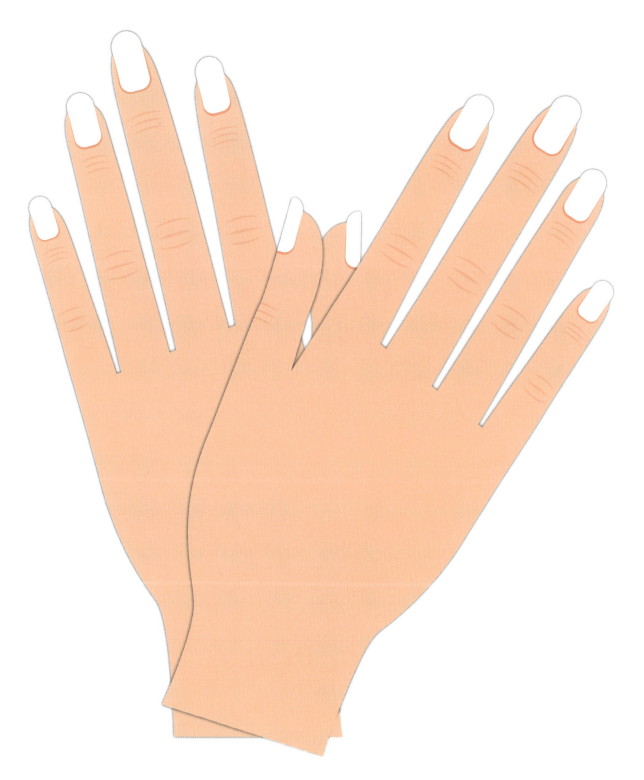

RAINBOW RESISTANCE

Someone with no regard for the order of the rainbow moved four colored pencils out of sequence in the image below. Can you find them and circle them so that order once again prevails over chaos?

CLOSET COMPULSION

Most of us aspire to a closet as organized as the one below, but look a little closer and you'll find a few hidden flaws. Find the five differences in the image at right and try to imagine a world in which you'd have an entire cubby dedicated to a throw pillow.

TWIN FOR THE WIN

In a perfect world, every sock would have a match. This puzzle provides you with that satisfying scenario. All you have to do is identify each sock's match by writing the number of the first sock next to its twin.

DECORATOR'S DREAM

A fresh layer of smooth icing is the canvas that makes a cake decorator's dreams come true.
Turn this blank canvas into a masterpiece for any occasion by drawing on your decorative touches.

COLOR CURE: TRIANGULAR

Add some grandeur to this exquisite geometric design with your favorite array of colors.
Frame and display your finished work for all to admire.

HAVE TO HALF

Love a good challenge? Use your keen eye and love of symmetry to draw the other half of this elegant string instrument.

ALL BUSINESS

The desk at left belongs to someone who takes pride in their job and their desktop organizing. The desk at right shows what happens when normal people interfere. Find the five changes in the image at right, circle them, and breathe a sigh of relief.

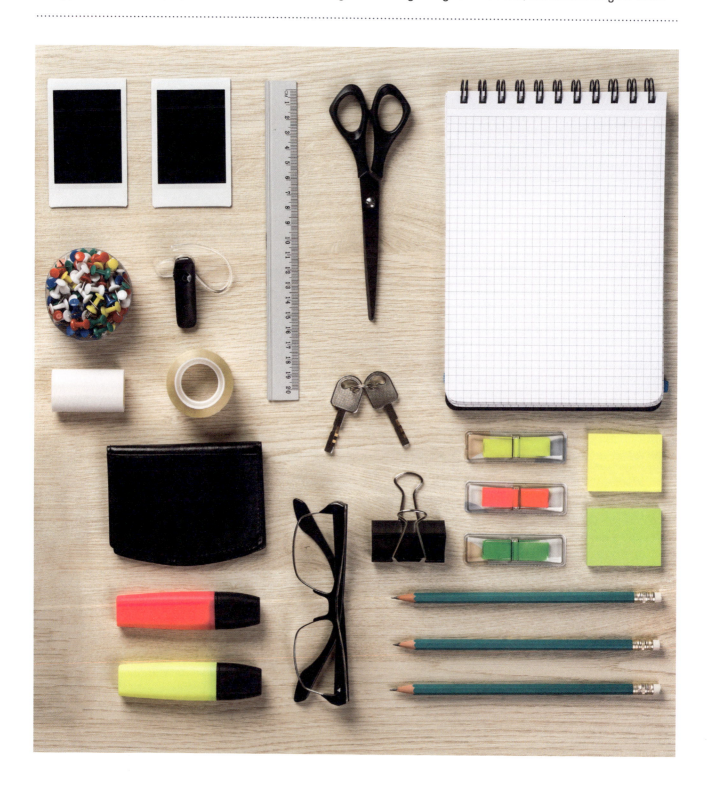

COLOR CURE: BLOOM

Even nature can't emulate this level of perfection. Let your artistic side blossom as
you shade this geometrically enhanced flower in all the latest colors.

BIRTHDAY BLOWOUT

You've planned the perfect party, made the perfect cake, and lined up just the right amount of candles in neat rows. All that's left to do is find and circle the three candles that blew out, sing the birthday song in perfect harmony, and call this party a success.

....

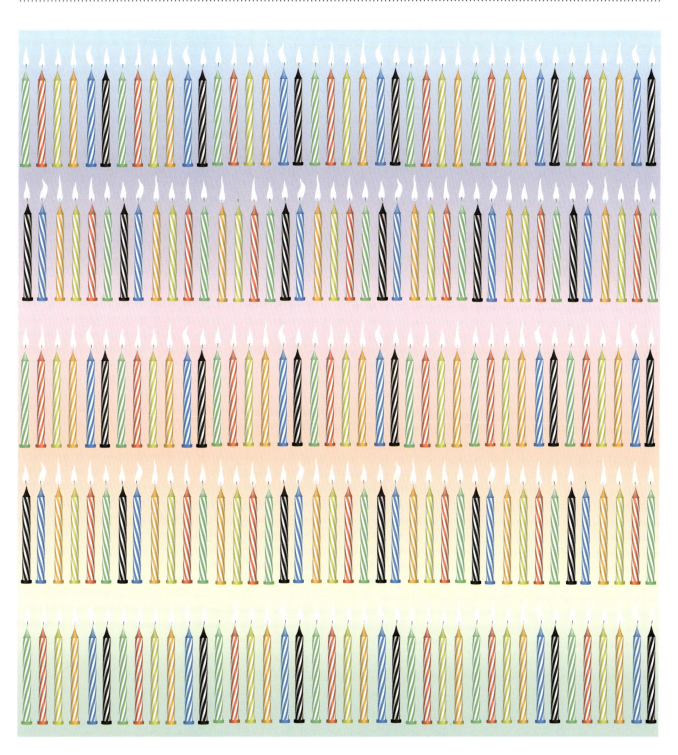

COLOR CURE: MOTIF

Stare deeply into this pattern until you can make sense of it, and make it your own with a strategic addition of color.

GARDEN QUEST

As enchanting as a garden labyrinth, this maze will lure you in. Only a mastermind like you can maneuver its intricate pathways. Stay calm and collected as you wander your way from start to finish.

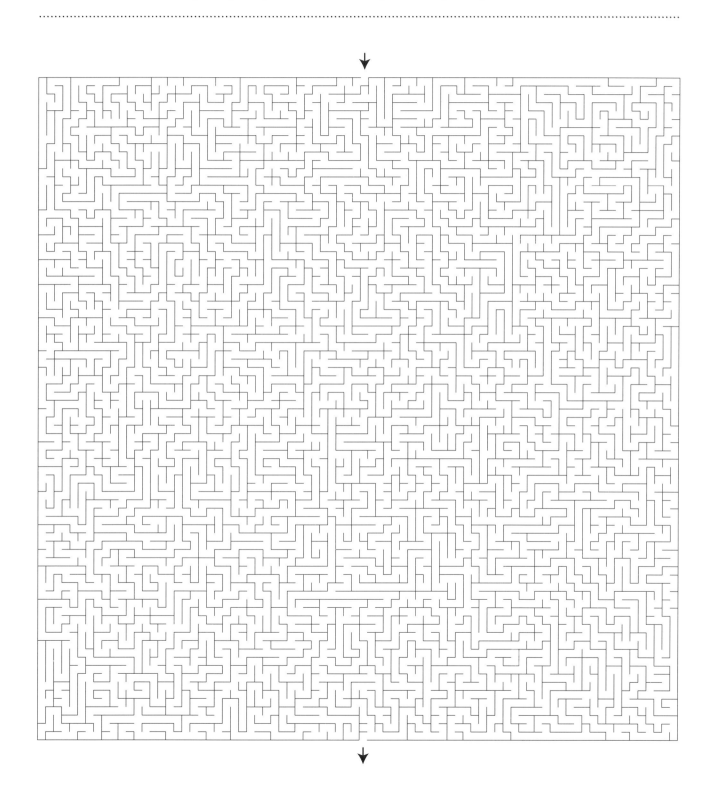

COLOR CURE: WAVES

Style doesn't take a day off. Tame this hypnotic design with a lovely touch of color.

CONNECT THE DOTS

Complete this dot-to-dot puzzle to pay tribute to the household item that makes perfect hair days possible.

BUBBLE POP

Simulate the tactile pleasure and satisfaction of popping bubble wrap with this interactive activity page. Just tap your pencil gently in the center of each round orb and make a dot. Imagine the thrill of popping each one. Pure heaven.

FLIGHT OF FANCY

Nature is full of eye-pleasing spectacles. The butterfly is a stunning example. Bring perfect symmetry to this garden goddess as you carefully color its left wing to match its right.

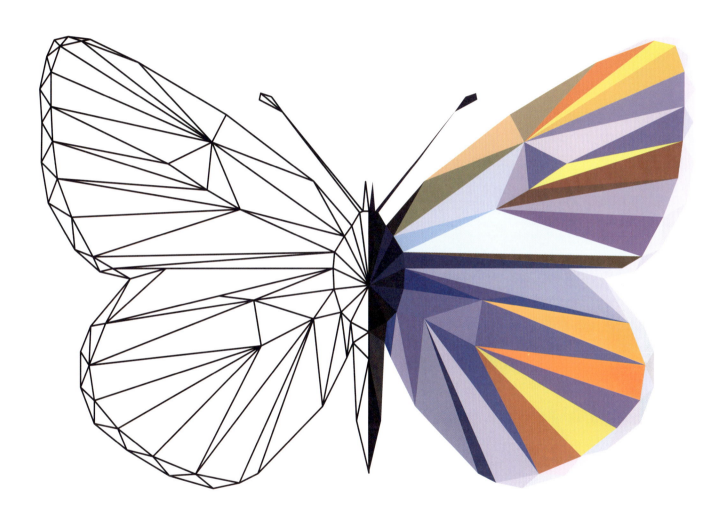

CONNECT THE DOTS

Finish this dot-to-dot puzzle to discover a household tool that gives you even more control (yes!) over your morning ritual.

ORDER IS KEY

This assortment of antiques is full of matching keys, with five stubborn exceptions.
Find the five keys that have no match and circle them to ensure that harmony and order win again.

SAY CHEESE

Family photos are an opportunity to present a shining example of your family at their best.
That said, a good photo-editing program can go a long way. This flawless family was edited to perfection in the image at left.
Compare it to the original photo at right and circle the five differences.

CONNECT THE DOTS

Everything goes more smoothly when you're armed with one of these.
Complete this dot-to-dot puzzle and honor one of the greatest inventions known to perfectionists.

STUCK ON YOU

Sticky notes make all things possible. Whether it's labeling boxes, flagging your favorite page of a book, or letting someone know that those leftovers in the fridge are off-limits, these happy little squares are like miniature personal assistants. To complete this sticky-note challenge, find the five pads of sticky notes that have started to peel (and make a note to order some more).

GARDEN GLORY

You hired a professional landscaper to emulate the beautiful flowerbed shown at left. She did a respectable job, with the exception of five differences. Find the differences between the two images and circle them—because excellence doesn't take a day off.

EVERYTHING IN ITS PLACE

Test your supreme puzzle-solving skills with this jigsaw challenge. Find the three pieces that settle effortlessly into place and draw an arrow where they belong to make this swirling design whole again.

UNFINISHED BUSINESS

Time is a horrifying jumble of moments until you arrange it neatly into a pleasing, sequential array of dates and days. Find and fix the six printing flaws in this faulty calendar (white out required!) so it can lead you effortlessly through the business of another year.

01 JAN

		1	2	3	4	5
6	7	8	9	10	11	12
13	14	15	16	17	18	19
20	21	22	23	24	25	26
27	28	29	30	31		

02 FEB

					1	2
3	4	5	5	7	8	9
10	11	12	13	14	15	16
17	18	19	20	21	22	23
24	25	26	27	28		

03 MAR

					1	2
3	4	5	6	7	8	9
10	11	12	13	14	15	16
17	18	19	20	21	22	23
24	25	26	27	28	29	30

04 APR

	1	2	3	4	5	6
7	8	9	10	11	12	13
14	15	16	17	18	19	20
21	22	23	24	25	26	27
28	29	30				

05 MAY

			1	2	3	4
5	6	7	8	9	10	11
12	13	14	15	16	17	18
19	24	21	22	23	24	25
26	27	28	29	30	31	

06 JUN

						1
2	3	4	5	6	7	8
9	10	11	12	13	14	15
16	17	18	19	20	21	22
23	24	25	26	27	28	29
30						

07 JUL

	1	2	3	4	5	6
7	8	9	11	10	12	13
14	15	16	17	18	19	20
21	22	23	24	25	26	27
28	29	30				

08 AUG

				1	2	3
4	5	6	7	8	9	10
11	12	13	14	15	16	17
18	19	20	21	22	23	24
25	26	27	28	29	30	31

09 SEP

1	2	3	4	5	6	7
8	9	10	11	12	13	14
15	16	17	18	19	20	21
22	23	24	25	26	27	28
29	30					

10 OCT

		1	2	3	4	5
6	7	8	9	10	11	12
13	14	15	16	17	18	19
20	21	22	23	24	25	26
27	28	29	30	31		

11 NOV

					1	2
3	4	5	6	8	8	9
10	11	12	13	14	15	16
17	18	19	20	21	22	23
24	25	26	27	28	29	30

12 DEC

1	2	3	4	5	6	7
8	9	10	11	12	13	14
15	16	17	18	19	20	21
22	23	24	25	26	27	28
29	30	31				

IN PERFECT SHAPE

Who says artists have to improvise? Shade in the other half of this panda using the completed half as your guide.

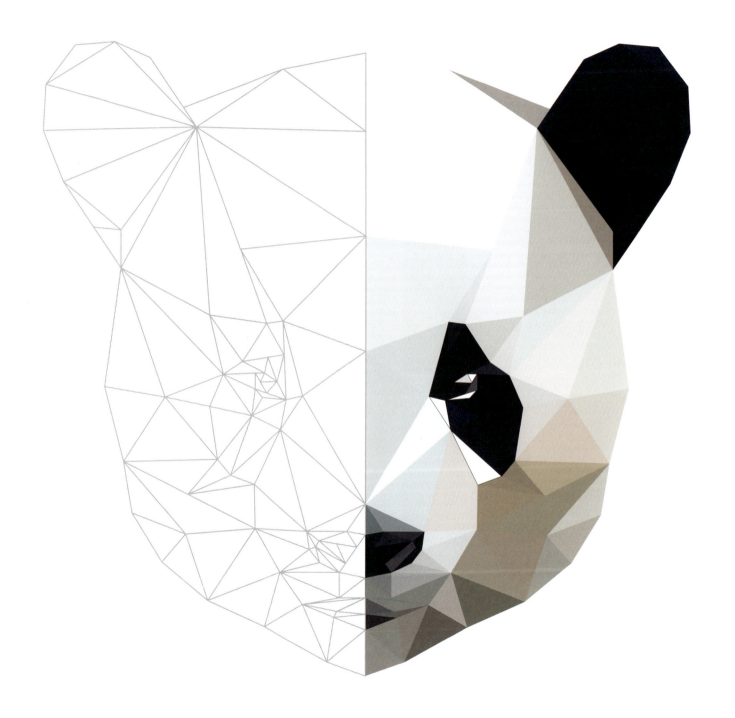

MAKE LIKE A LIBRARIAN

Books can contain wild stories and runaway thoughts into tidy little paper packages. For that reason, they're worthy of special love and attention. Add the titles of the 30 books below in alphabetical order (as if you had to be told!) along the book spines. Note: Ignore articles like *The*, just like a real librarian.

Atlas Shrugged · Beloved · Bleak House · Candide · Crime and Punishment
Dubliners · Hamlet · Heart of Darkness · Invisible Man · Ivanhoe
Leaves of Grass · Lolita · Metamorphoses · Moby Dick · Poems of Emily Dickinson
Sons and Lovers · The Call of the Wild · The Grapes of Wrath · The Great Gatsby · The Iliad
The Joy Luck Club · The Jungle · The Stranger · The Tempest · The Time Machine
The Wind in the Willows · Treasure Island · Ulysses · Waiting for Godot · War and Peace

HOME IMPROVEMENT

The online listing on the left shows a house with curb appeal that won't quit. But when you pull up to see it in person, your thorough inspection will uncover five small, but important, differences. Circle the differences in the house on the right and use your findings to haggle for a lower price.

CONNECT THE DOTS

It'll be there by your side whenever dust and dirt keep you from living your best life.
Solve this dot-to-dot puzzle to complete the image of a germophobe's best friend.

DANDELION DREAMS

There are a whole lot of bright yellow dandelions in this field ready to grant your every wish.
(Be grateful that these happy little weeds are here instead of taking over your perfectly manicured yard.)
Count the number of yellow dandelions in every stage of bloom and write the number here:

_____ .

MIRROR MOSAIC

Give this puzzle the gift of its other half by coloring in the white squares to mirror the pattern on the left. Symmetry prevails!

OFF TO BED

Extinguishing all the lights in your home is a satisfying way to end the day. Find the five light switches that haven't yet been turned off and make way for a restful night of sleep.

BURNER ON THE BRAIN

We've all left the house only to wonder if we forgot to turn the burner off. This little puzzle will assure you that you've got it handled. Correct this dangerous situation below by circling the burners (there are five) that need to be turned off.

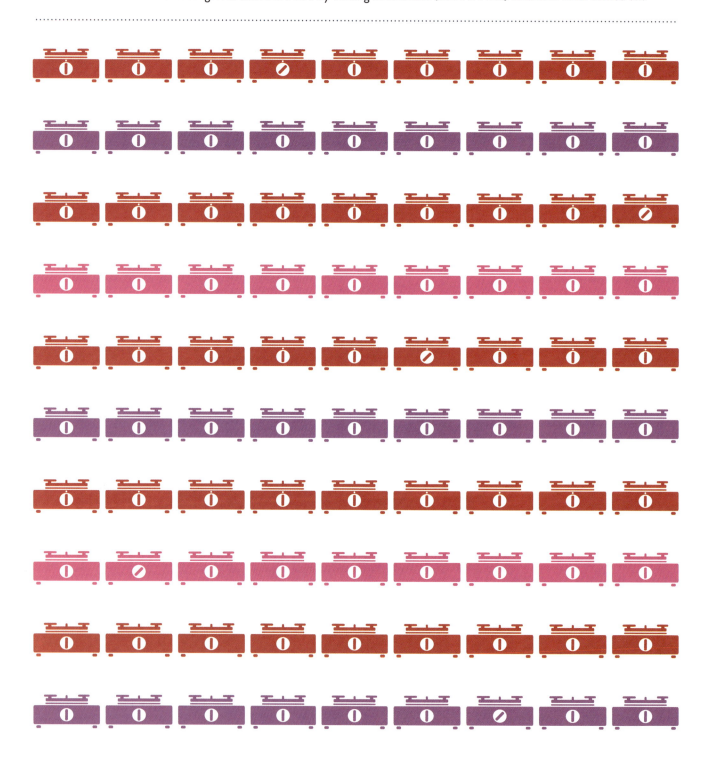

BOTTOMS UP

One too many martinis has you feeling as off-balanced as these glasses. Steady yourself by counting the stemware stacked precariously inside the larger one. Write the number here:

_____ .

SHADOW WARP

Take a break from perfecting your serve to identify and circle the five tennis balls with warped shadows below. Even the sun has to adhere to the rules!

CONNECT THE DOTS

Neat freaks often form an attachment to this magical device, though it comes with a few of its own. Connect the dots to find out what it is.

NEW AND IMPROVED

If you look closely, you'll notice that this farmhouse cupboard transformed from shabby (left) to chic (right).
Use your power of perception to find the five little changes that brought about this makeover.

ANY WAY YOU SLICE IT

Don't let a few inconsistent slices ruin your picnic. Circle the five melon slices below that have the "wrong" number of seeds and feel good knowing you've saved the world from the threat of chaos.

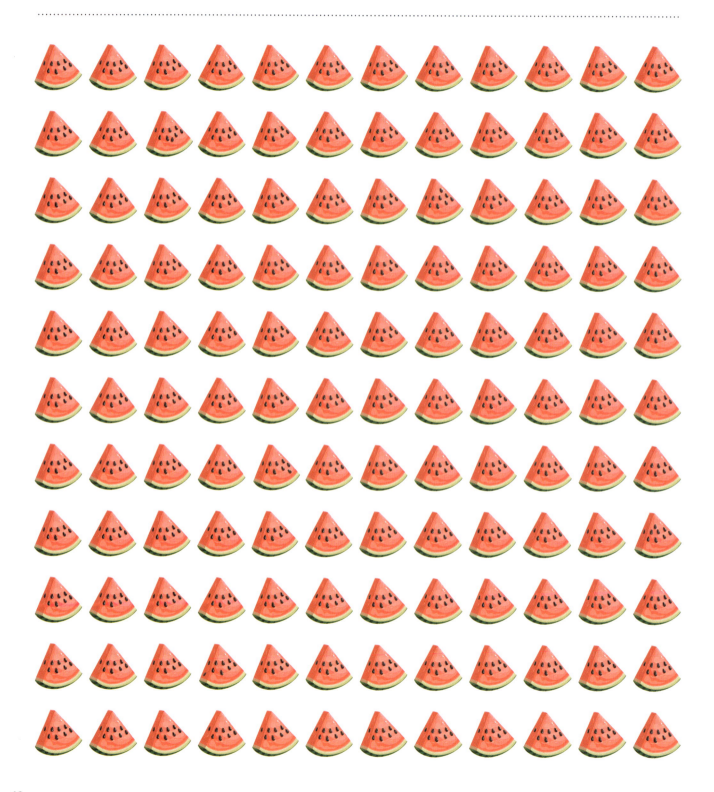

MIRROR MOSAIC II

Give your colored pencils a sense of purpose today. Complete this mosaic by coloring in the white squares on the bottom half to mirror the pattern shown on the top half.

SCREEN PRISTINE

Take the cell phone screen protector challenge and practice applying a screen cover without causing those dreaded air bubbles. Number the steps below in correct order from 1 to 6 to prove that you've got it handled.

COLOR CURE

When life gets frustrating and unpredictable, a repeating design is a welcome reminder that some things go just as expected. Stay safely inside the lines as you color this soothing image in your favorite hues.

PIECES ALL AROUND

Test your supreme puzzle-solving skills with this jigsaw challenge. Find the four pieces that will end the madness of an unfinished puzzle and draw an arrow where each one belongs.

DRESS YOUR SHELF

A bookshelf organized by color makes a striking statement. Follow the lead of the first book on each shelf and shade in the spines of the books to the right until you've created a magnificent spectrum of orderliness.

MIND YOUR Qs

It's up to you to restore order in what should otherwise be a soothing sequence of uninterrupted Qs below.
Find the five Os that snuck in and wreaked havoc all over this page and circle them. Then forget this ever happened.

QQQQQQQQQQQQQQQQQQQQQQQQQ
QQQQQQQQQQQQQQQQQQQQQQQQQ
QQQQQQQQQQQQQQQQQQQQQQQQQ
QQQQQQQQQQQQQQQQQQQQQQQQQ
QQQQQQQQQQQQQQQQQQQQQQQQQ
QQQQQQQQQQQQQQQQQQQQQQQQQ
QQQQQQQQQQQQQQQQQQQQQQQQQ
QQQQQQQQQQQQQQQQQQQQQQQQQ
QQQQQQQQQQQQQQQQQQQQQQQQQ
QQQQQQQQQQQQQQQQQQQQQQQQQ
QQQQQQQQQQQQQQQQQQQQQQQQQ
QQQQQQQQQOQQQQQQQQQQQQQQQ
QQQQQQQQQQQQQQQQQQQQQQQQQ
QQQQQQQQQQQQQQQQQQQQQQQQQ
QQQQQQQQQQQQQQQQQQQQQQQQQ
QQQQQQQQQQQQQQQQQQQQQQQQQ
QQQQQQQQQQQQQQQQQQQQQQQQOQ
QQQQQQQQQQQQQQQQQQQQQQQQQ
QQQQQQQQQQQQQQQQQQQQQQQQQ
QQQQQQQQQQQQQQQQQQQQQQQQQ
QQQQQQQQQQQQQQQQQQQQQQQQQ
QQQQQQQQQQQQQQQQQQQQQQQQQ
QOQQQQQQQQQQQQQQQQQQQQQQQ
QQQQQQQQQQQQQQQQQQQQQQQOQ

SEEDS OF PROGRESS

Enjoy counting the floating seeds in this puzzle without aggravating your allergies. Think of each seed as a brilliant idea you'll one day make happen and write the total number here:

_____ .

ON A ROLL

Try not to lose your marbles as you sort out which five of these colorful little orbs is different in the picture on the right. Circle the differences and let the good times roll.

FIND YOUR PIECE II

Add a moment of pure satisfaction to your day when you find the one shape below that (without being moved or flipped) will complete this image. Circle it and start to feel whole again.

MAKE A POINT

For type As, neat freaks, and anyone else with standards, an unsharpened pencil is a thing of shame and untapped potential. Don't let the blunt ends below spoil your good mood. Draw them in as sharp as you can and fill the world with hope and possibility.

FRESH FINDS

Whether it's placed neatly on your pillow or offered politely by a loved one, the peppermint provides socially acceptable breath when you need it most. Find the five mints below that have an odd number of stripes, and circle them.

ROLL AGAIN

Take a look at the random rolls below and find the five dice that are not regulation standard: each has one blank side. Circle the offending dice and banish them from play forever.

CHILD'S PLAY

Nothing wreaks havoc and disorder with more efficiency than a child, so a clean playroom is truly a wonder to behold. Before you envy this impeccable family and their seemingly type A offspring, take a gander at the image on the right, which reflects five key differences after a wild day of horseplay.

JUST MY LUCK

Show off your dogged determination as you search for the five lucky four-leaf clovers hidden in
this scattered pile of substandard ones. Circle them knowing you were born a winner.

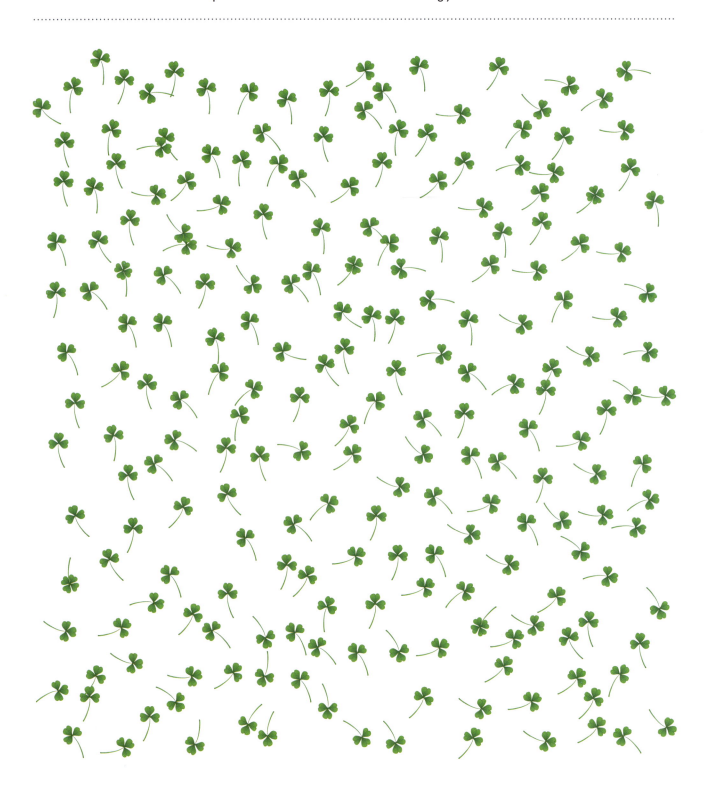

ONE OF A KIND

This dealer did not know when to hold 'em. He mixed in an extra deck and now there are duplicates everywhere. Find the five cards that don't have matches before you report him to management.

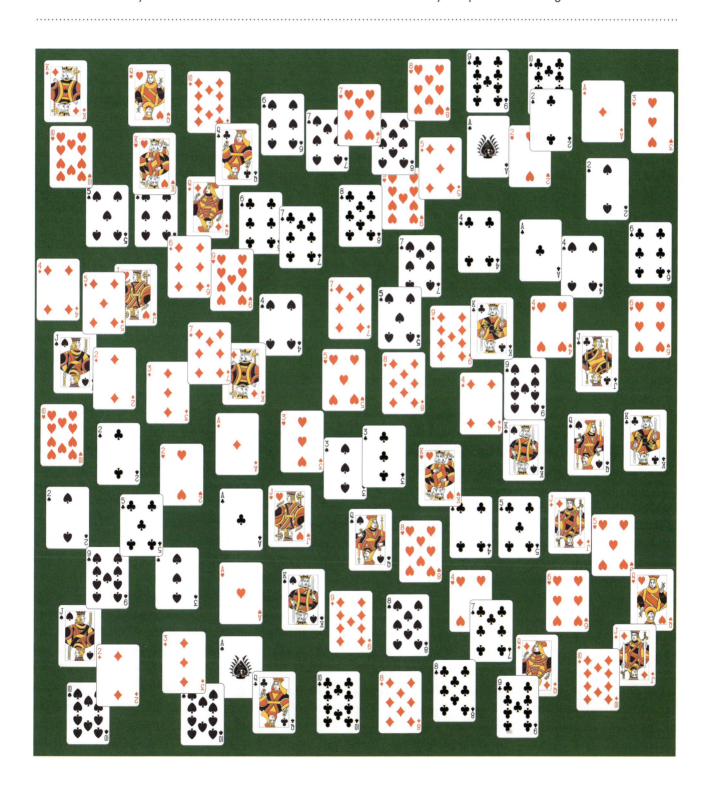

COLOR CURE: ZIGZAG

No one's brain is busier than yours, so when life offers you a coloring break—go ahead and take it!
Set aside your to-do list, grab your markers or pencils, and give your tired mind the vacation it deserves.

A LOT OF FUN

To some, a good parking job is a sight to behold; a work of art. It displays a keen sense of spatial awareness, expert hand-eye coordination, and the tireless pursuit of perfection. While backing into a spot is one of the higher forms of this art, uniformity reigns supreme. Find the five cars that are parked in a different direction and circle them.

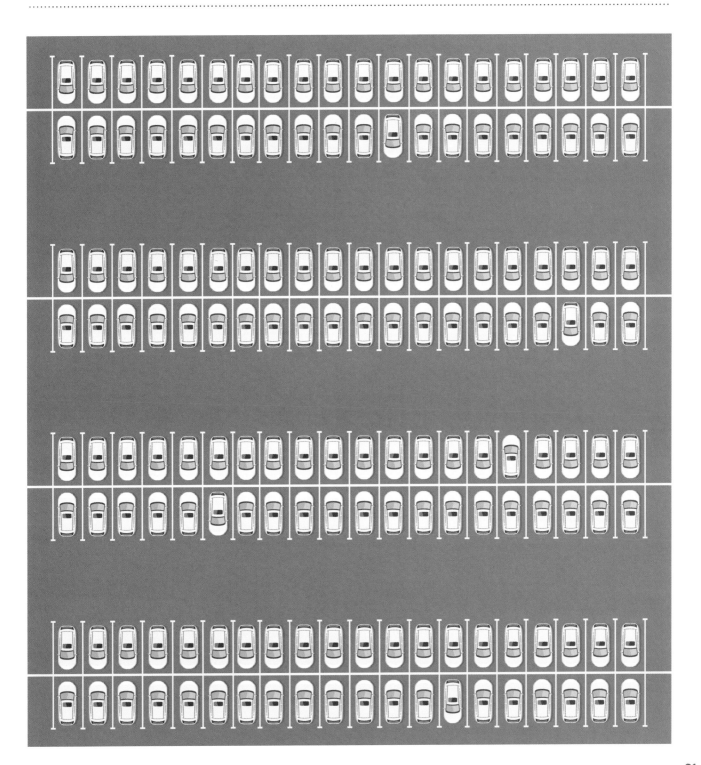

RESORT TO THIS

You may have had one too many mai tais, but finding variations in these vacation photos is challenging. Circle the five differences in the image on the right and then move on to the next activity in your detailed vacation itinerary. Relaxing is overrated.

FULL CIRCLE

This circular maze is almost as beautiful and intricate as the workings of your highly systematic mind. Use your brain power and determination to master this puzzle and emerge triumphant on the other side.

ON THE DOT

Whether they're aligned in neat standing rows, matched into pairs, or making that satisfying clacking sound, dominoes can really rouse the type A's spirit. Bring order to this array of toppled dominoes by circling any that don't have an exact match.

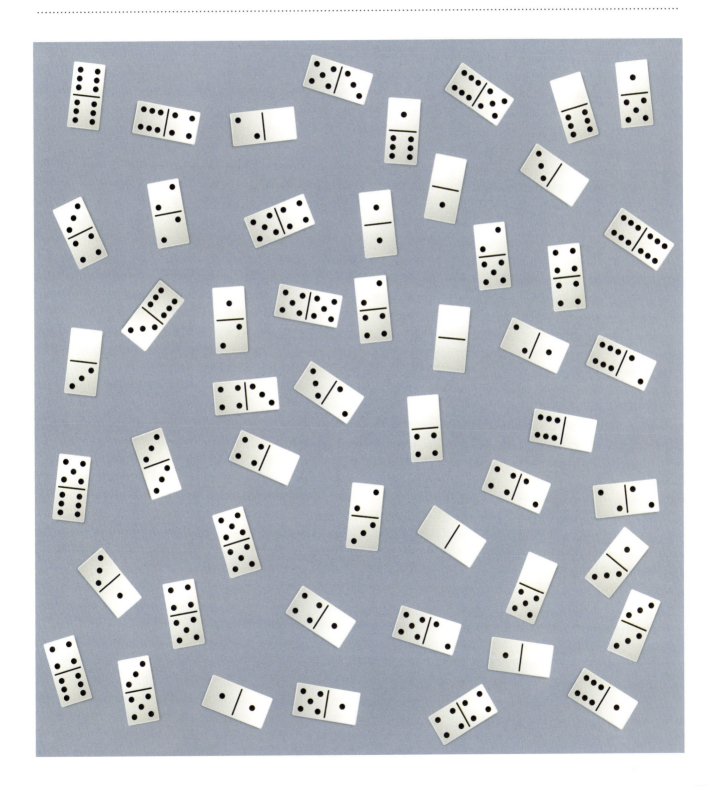

FOOT WEAR AND TEAR

Bask in the simple splendor of a shoe organizer done right. Then hunt down the five differences in the image at right and resolve to heal the world of imperfection, one flawed piece of footwear at a time.

CONNECT THE DOTS

Some things are best accomplished by someone with an eye for detail and patience for perfection. Solve this dot-to-dot puzzle to discover a meticulously-crafted miracle.

DUCK AND CROSS

Scoot under and cross over the narrow bridges of this challenging maze. Make your way expertly to the finish and pat yourself on the back for having accomplished what most could not.

WHAT THE HEX

Patience is a virtue when it comes to this intense, six-sided maze. Make your way through this puzzle to prove you have what it takes. Do it without throwing your pencil across the room and bonus points are in order.

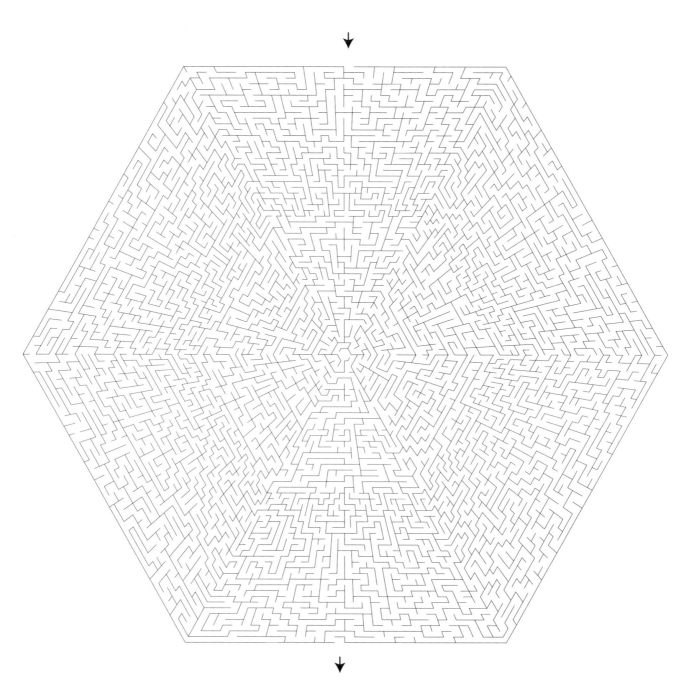

DAIQUIRI DILEMMA

You asked for your usuals, but a few of these drinks look different to you. Identify and circle the five cocktails that feature unexpected garnish or different color ingredients and send them back. Life's too short for compromise.

IN-SPA-RATION

Nothing soothes and satisfies the mind and soul like a spa day, complete with fresh towels, aromatic orchids, and a relaxing hot stone massage. Treat yourself to a rewarding challenge as you compare the two images below and circle the five differences in the image at right.

GRAMMAR POLICE

If the grammar police were on patrol, this puzzle would be under arrest. Find the five punctuation marks that don't belong and circle them as if the integrity of the English language depended on it.

WIGGLE ON THROUGH

Laugh in the face of this wiggly maze challenge knowing you'll crush this goal like you do all others. Then pin some new goals to your vision board and crush them, too.

YOUR MOVE

It's the first day of chess club and things are off to a bad start: There are too many of some pieces and not enough of others. Find and circle the chess piece that appears only four times (in the same color) and resolve to join a new club.

TRICKY TILES

No one can play this game of mah-jongg until the tiles appearing only once in this set are identified and circled.
Only then can you match up common suits and work your way to victory with a satisfying declaration of *sik wu*!

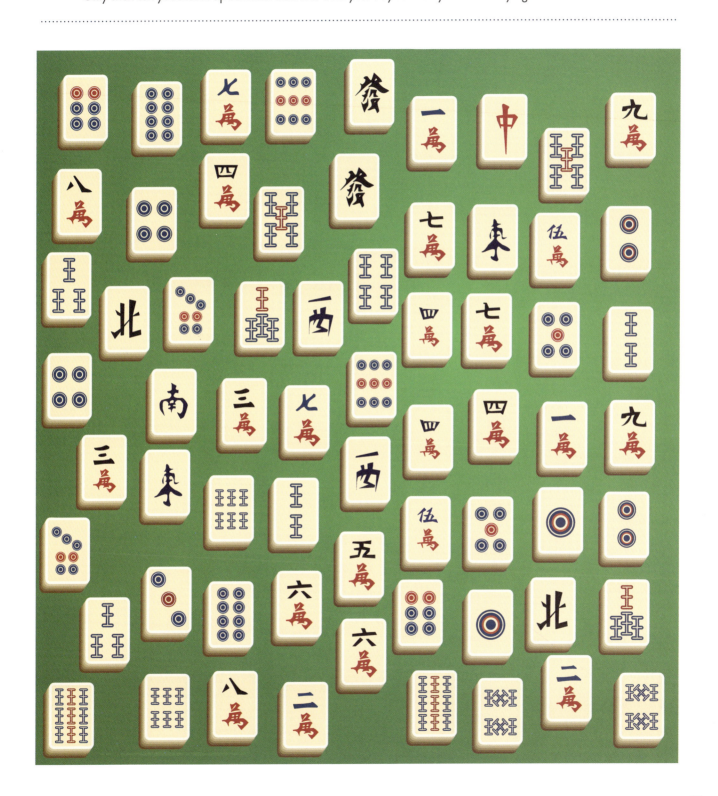

BUILDERS BEWARE

Chaos ensues when a few orange Legos are carelessly dropped into the yellow lego bin at right.
Restore order by identifying the imposter bricks and circling them. Then try to forget this ever happened.

ALPHA-THREAT

You'll never make a game-winning word if you keep drawing the same letter tile. Find the letter that appears most in this collection and circle it so you can steer clear and guarantee another glorifying victory.

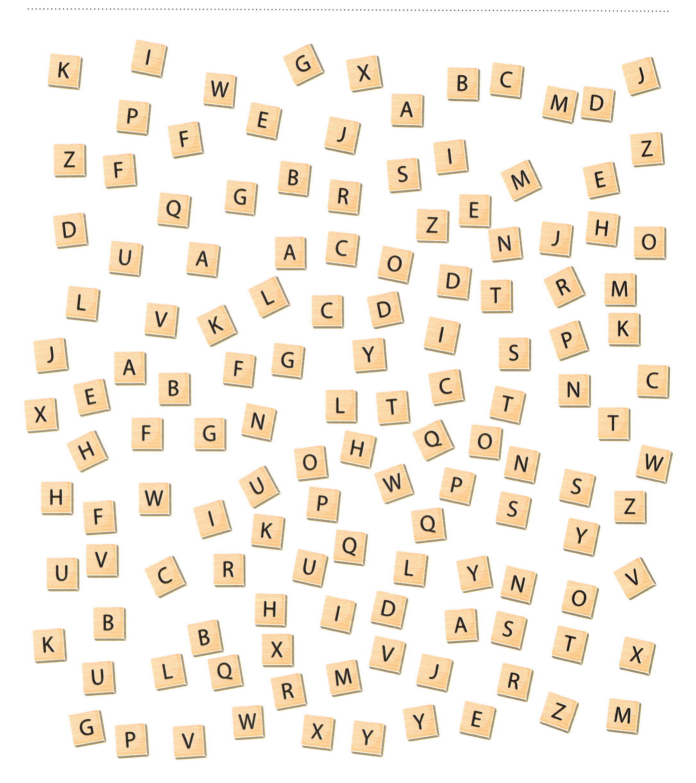

FREAKS OF NATURE

Long walks on the beach collecting shells sounds relaxing. Unless you're a type A with a compulsion to then arrange those shells into perfectly patterned sets. Find the five slight variations in shell types within this carefully curated collection and chuck them back out to sea.

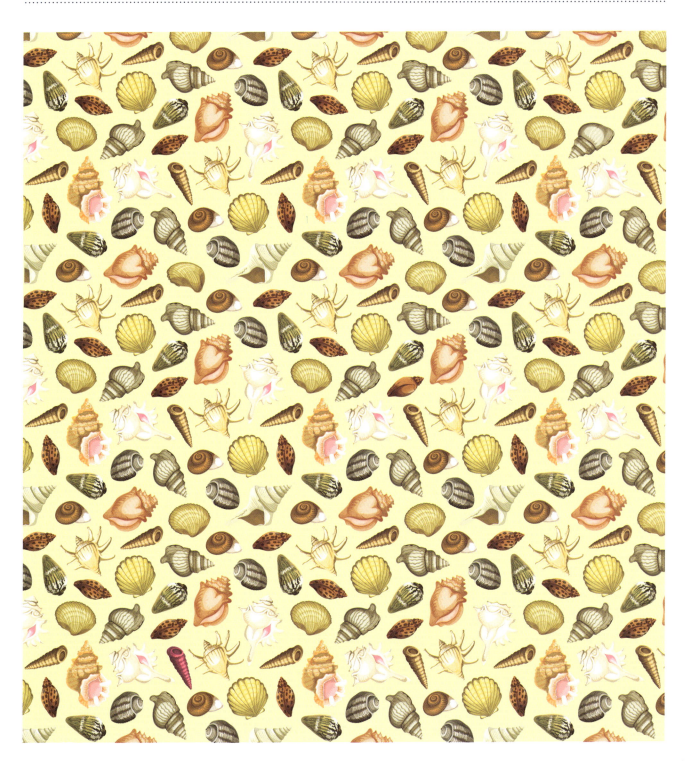

PIECE OF CAKE

No pressure, but this day had better be perfect. The only way to ensure that it's a success is to find and circle the five changes in the wedding cake at right before the bride sees them and calls the whole thing off.

ANSWER KEY

Page 4 - Dot Your i's and Cross Your t's

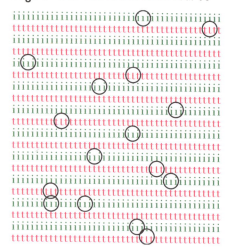

Page 5 - Go Green

Page 6 - I Spy Disorder

Page 8 - Find Your Piece

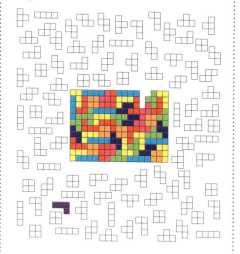

Page 9 - Hostess with the Most-est

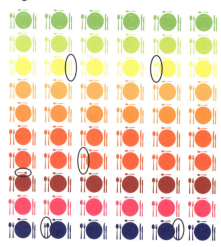

Page 10 - Catch the Rainbows

Page 11 - Pour Favor

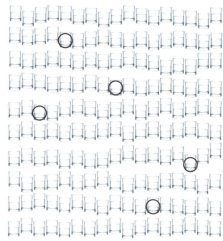

Page 12 - Take Charge

Page 13 - A Place for Everyone

Page 14 - Confection Perfection

Page 17 - Making Arrangements

Page 18 - Drawn to Perfection

Page 19 - Cool Beans

237 JELLY BEANS

Page 21 - Rainbow Resistance

Page 22 - Closet Compulsion

Page 24 - Twin for the Win

Page 27 - Have to Half

Page 28 - All Business

Page 31 - Birthday Blowout

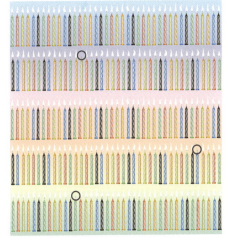

Page 33 - Garden Quest

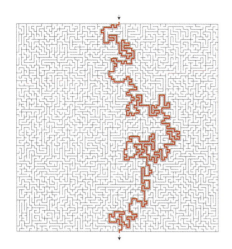

Page 35 - Connect the Dots

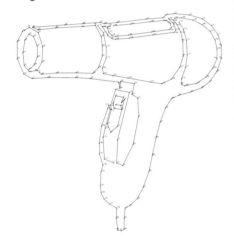

Page 37 - Flight of Fancy

Page 38 - Connect the Dots

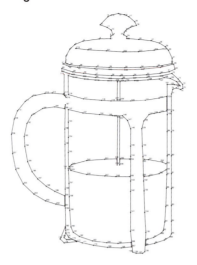

Page 39 - Order Is Key

Page 40 - Say Cheese

Page 42 - Connect the Dots

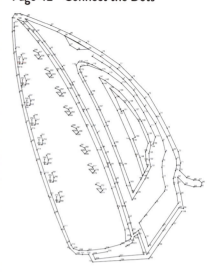

Page 43 - Stuck on You

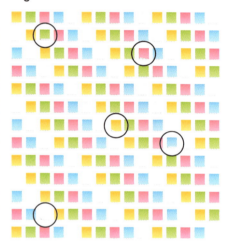

Page 44 - Garden Glory

Page 46 - Everything in its Place

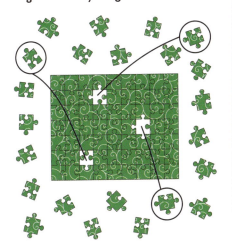

Page 47 - Unfinished Business

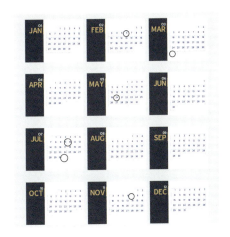

Page 48 - In Perfect Shape

Page 49 - Make Like a Librarian

Page 50 - Home Improvement

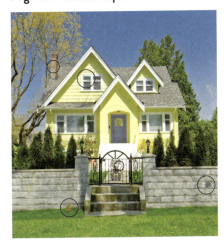

Page 52 - Connect the Dots

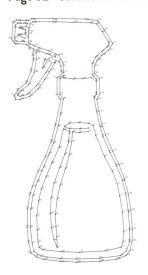

Page 53 - Dandelion Dreams

139 DANDELIONS

Page 54 - Mirror Mosaic

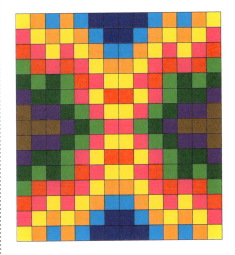

Page 55 - Off to Bed

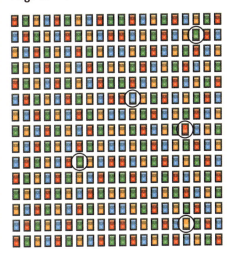

Page 56 - Burner on the Brain

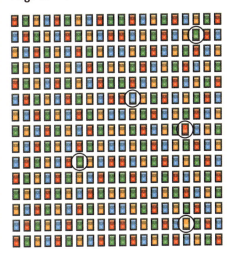

Page 57 - Bottoms Up

138 GLASSES

Page 58 - Shadow Warp

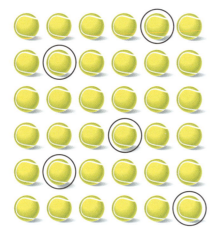

Page 59 - Connect the Dots

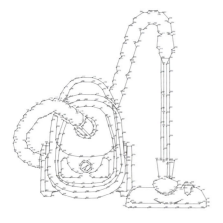

Page 60 - New and Improved

Page 62 - Any Way You Slice It

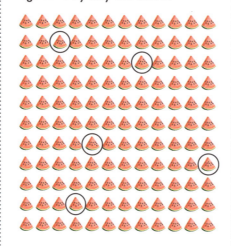

Page 63 - Mirror Mosaic II

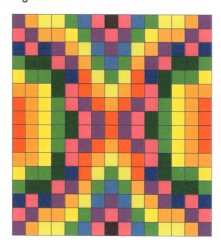

Page 64 - Screen Pristine

Page 66 - Pieces All Around

Page 67 - Dress Your Shelf

Page 68 - Mind Your Qs

Page 69 - Seeds of Progress

277 SEEDS

Page 70 - On a Roll

Page 72 - Find Your Piece II

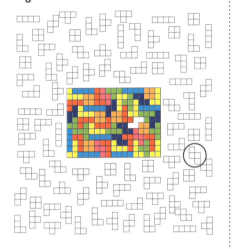

Page 73 - Make a Point

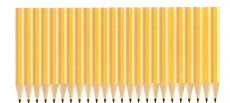

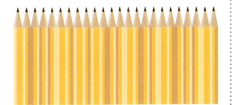

Page 74 - Fresh Finds

Page 75 - Roll Again

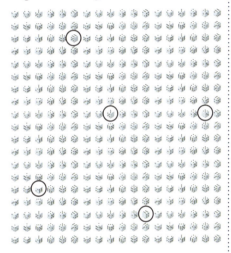

Page 76 - Child's Play

Page 78 - Just My Luck

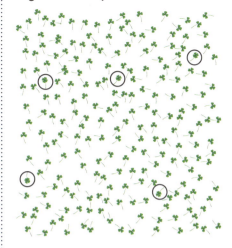

Page 79 - One of a Kind

Page 81 - A Lot of Fun

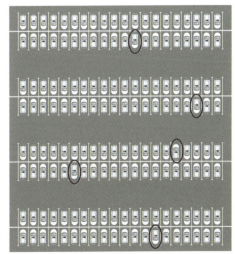

Page 82 - Resort to This

Page 84 - Full Circle

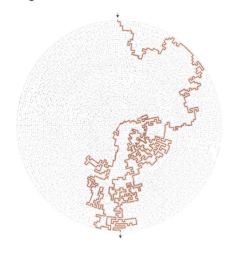

Page 85 - On the Dot

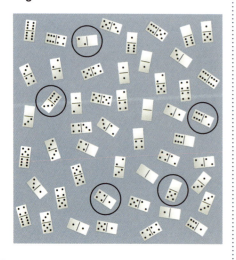

Page 86 - Foot Wear and Tear

Page 88 - Connect the Dots

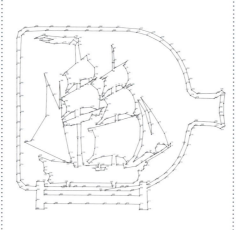

Page 89 - Duck and Cross

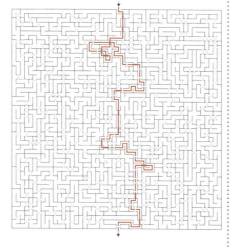

Page 90 - What the Hex

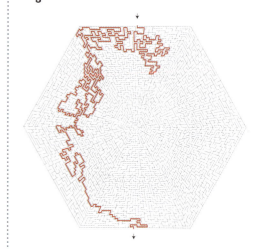

Page 91 - Daiquiri Dilemma

Page 92 - In-spa-ration

Page 94 - Grammar Police

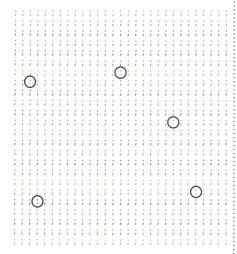

Page 95 - Wiggle on Through

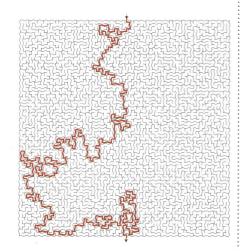

Page 96 - Your Move

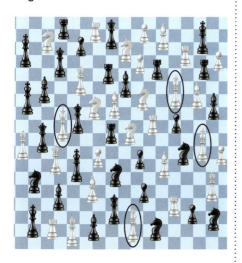

Page 97 - Tricky Tiles

Page 98 - Builders Beware

Page 100 - Alpha-threat

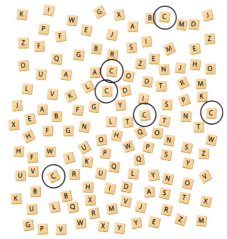

Page 101 - Freaks of Nature

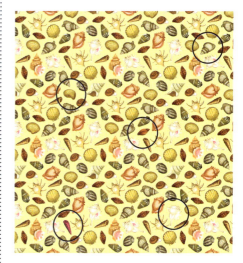

Page 102 - Piece of Cake